Free Indeed

David & Barbara CERULLO

ISBN1-887600-69-8

Printed in the USA

TABLE
of Contents

INTRODUCTION

God doesn't promise a life without problems.

But regardless of what's going on around you or in the world, you can know the freedom of being surrounded and safeguarded by God's Presence, peace, and protection:

"If the Son makes you free, you shall be free indeed."
– JOHN 8:36

Peace of God will guard your mind…"Guard" is an interesting word for Paul to use. It's a military term that implies your mind is a battle zone and needs to be protected.

The purpose of a guard is usually to prevent a hostile invasion or to keep someone from escaping. The peace of God operates in the same way. God's peace will keep you focused on His truth and guard your mind from external negative influences and the devil who wishes to bring fear into your life.

Lean into the safety and security of God's Word, His truth, and His arms of love and compassion, where you will be comforted and encouraged.

Pray about your circumstances instead of worrying about them. Commit your problems to God in prayer, trusting that He will provide deliverance.

God's Word reminds us: *"Trust in the Lord with all your heart, and lean not on your own understanding; in all your ways acknowledge Him, and He shall direct your paths," (Proverbs 3:5-6).*

God loves you. You never need to doubt His safety and protection. When your faith needs strengthening…when you need courage and peace…when you need wisdom to know what to do…draw on the Word of God to bless and encourage you. There you will find wisdom and strength that comforts, counsels, guides, directs, and teaches you.

As you read these devotions, invite the Holy Spirit to supernaturally impart God's peace into your mind, soul, and spirit. Allow these verses to soak into your very being.

You will find as the Psalmist David said, *"Thy Word is a lamp unto my feet and a light unto my path."*

Barbara and I pray that these words will strengthen and comfort you through any challenging circumstances you may face.

We would be honored to join with you in the Prayer of Faith. Please contact our anointed prayer ministers at Prayer@inspiration.org any time you need for us to agree with you in prayer.

Remember this...God has not planned any defeats for you. He wants you to be *Free Indeed!*

David & Barbara

David and Barbara Cerullo
Inspiration Ministries

EVERY DAY
in Grace

Port in a Storm

hen huge cargo ships enter a river on their way to a port city, they take on an experienced River Pilot. The Pilot guides the multimillion-dollar vessel safely to port because he knows the only secure passage through all the shifting sandbars and all the rocks and snags that could endanger the ship.

Friend, Proverbs 3:5-6 tells us that God Himself is <u>our</u> River Pilot: *"Trust in the Lord with all your heart; do not depend on your own understanding. Seek His will in all you do, and He will direct your paths."*

When life gets confusing and uncertain, call on the Lord—He knows the way to go—He will get you safely home.

---

*Father, only You know the way
through all of the troubles and
confusion of my life. I now put all of
my trust in You, and You alone.
Show me the way to go.
In Jesus' name. Amen.*

The Secret Formula

n the Dark Ages, men were always looking for a secret formula that would turn worthless lead into priceless gold. Friend, I've got a much better formula for you—one that turns tragedy into triumph, misery into hope, fear into joy.

That secret is found in Romans 8:28. ***"We know that in everything God works for the good of those who love Him, who have been called according to His purpose."***

No matter what problem you're facing, no matter how dark the road ahead, God is at work in those very circumstances. Trust Him to bring you through the difficult times and use them for your good.

I thank You, Father, that You use
even the bad things in my life
to bring about a greater good.
In Jesus' name. Amen.

The Journey From Head to Heart

Friend, the greatest adventure you'll ever have in this life is in moving the Word of God from your head into your feet. It's not a long journey, but if you make it, it'll change your life completely.

The roadmap is found in James 1:25: *"...he who looks into the perfect law of liberty and continues in it, and is not a forgetful hearer but a doer of the work, this one will be blessed in what he does."*

Most of us have read the Bible for years, heard countless sermons, read scores of Christian books. But until we can take all of that head knowledge and start really living it, it does no one any good.

---

*Father, teach me to be a doer
of Your Word; help me to take what I
believe and really start living it.
In Jesus' name. Amen.*

Leave the Driving to Him

There's a saying that is very old and very wise—you can't steer a parked car. The same is true of our lives—we want to know what God wants us to do, but very seldom does He just lay it out for us. We have to start moving, step out in faith, and give Him a chance to steer.

And Micah 6:8 is where you start: *"He has shown you, O man, what is good. And what does the Lord require of you? To act justly and to love mercy and to walk humbly with your God."*

Friend, you just need to start walking. Take a step in faith, and as long as you're doing the right thing, the just thing, God will take it from there.

Father, I now step out in faith.
I fully trust that You will steer me
in the direction I should go.
In Jesus' name. Amen.

Cosmic Intimacy

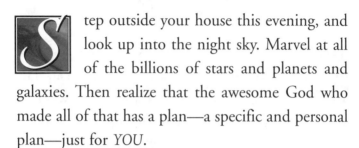

tep outside your house this evening, and look up into the night sky. Marvel at all of the billions of stars and planets and galaxies. Then realize that the awesome God who made all of that has a plan—a specific and personal plan—just for *YOU*.

He spells it out in Jeremiah 29:11: ***"I know the plans I have for you," declares the Lord, "plans to prosper you and not to harm you, plans to give you hope and a future."***

It's really that simple, my friend. The God of the universe wants to help *you,* to give you hope. He *personally* cares about your future. Let Him have His way—your life will never be the same.

Thank You, Father, that out of
all Your wondrous creation,
You care personally for me.
In Jesus' name. Amen.

The Last Word

here are a lot of people who seem to have control over our lives—from the boss at work to the judge in court, from the politicians to the lawyers.

But Proverbs 21:1 tells us that there is Someone else who *always* has the last word in deciding our case: ***"The king's heart is in the hand of the Lord, like the rivers of water; He turns it wherever He wishes."***

Whenever you need justice or a favorable decision, don't look to man for deliverance—turn to the King of kings—<u>all</u> authority is in His capable hands.

Father, thank You that You are
the Head of all authority over me,
and that justice comes from You.
Thank You for being in control
of the circumstances in my life.
In Jesus' name. Amen.

I Spy

 hese days, surveillance cameras are every-where—in ATM machines, on the streets, inside stores and malls. But how would you react if your every act—both public *and* private— were being videotaped for all to see?

Consider the words of Ecclesiastes 12:14: *"God will bring every deed into judgment, including every hidden thing, whether it is good or evil."*

God is watching, friend—not to try and catch us in some sin, but as a loving, concerned parent— just the way you watch out for *your* children and want the best for them.

Help me to remember
that You are always looking out
for me, Father, and to behave
only in ways that will please You.
In Jesus' name. Amen.

Small Sins, Big Consequences

s there any difference in God's eyes between robbing a bank and telling a little lie to your spouse? Is kidnapping any greater sin than "exaggerating" on your taxes?

Well, take a look at Romans 3:23, and then you tell me, friend. *"For all have sinned and fall short of the glory of God."*

We can't justify our behavior by claiming that it's just a small sin—that if nobody finds out about it, God will simply look the other way. There is no such thing as a "white lie." There's no "fudge factor" with God—sin is sin. Period.

Father, forgive me for my sins—
because all sin separates me from
You—and I don't want anything
to come between us.
In Jesus' name. Amen.

Change Your Clothes

hen your clothes get dirty, what do you do? Well, it's not rocket science—you change into clean clothes.

Ephesians 4:22 and 24 tells us of a more important change of wardrobe: *"With regard to your former way of life…put off your old self, which is being corrupted by its deceitful desires…and …put on the new self, created to be like God in true righteousness and holiness."*

Jesus paid the price for our sins—He has given us a brand new life. All we have to do is take off the old self like a dirty shirt and simply put on the clean royal robes of our new life.

Father, thank You that You
have done all the work for me—
You died for my sins, and all I have
to do is put on the clean new life
You have for me.
In Jesus' name. Amen.

Do You Know the Way?

hen you're hopelessly lost, the greatest thing is finding someone who can give you good directions. But where do you turn when you've lost your way in life?

Psalm 32:8 and Isaiah 30:21 have the roadmap. *"I will instruct you and teach you in the way you should go: I will counsel you and watch over you,"* and *"Whether you turn to the right or to the left, your ears will hear a voice behind you, saying, 'This is the way; walk in it.'"*

Friend, that's the best news possible if you've lost your way—God Himself will guide you home. All you have to do is ask Him for directions.

Lord, sometimes I feel lost
and don't know the way to go.
Please show me the way. Thank you.
In Jesus' name. Amen.

Stuff and Such

Have you ever thought about all the stuff that you stuff into your head? Names, dates, places, song lyrics, phone numbers, television commercials, trivia, memories, the names of the entire cast of *Gilligan's Island*... But how much of that stuff is really useful?

Psalm 119:11 talks about our priorities. ***"Your word I have hidden in my heart, that I might not sin against You!"***

Take control of the stuff you stuff into your head. Fill your mind...your thoughts...emotions with the Word of God. The benefits will change your life—and last for eternity.

———————— ✑ ————————

Lord, help me to guard
what I let into my head and
to fill my heart with Your Word.
In Jesus' name. Amen.

Twelve

Short but Sweet

t's the one verse in the Bible that every kid in Sunday School *wants* to memorize, and for one reason only—it's the shortest verse in the Bible:

John 11:35— *"Jesus wept."*

Yes, it's a great one to memorize—not to make points in a memory verse contest—but because that tiny two-word verse speaks volumes about our Lord. He is the King of all kings, the Lord of all lords, the creator of the heavens and the earth and all that is in them, yet He had such compassion for a single human being that...Jesus wept.

And friend, He has that very same concern for you—personally and individually.

Father, I am in awe of
Your wondrous love for me.
Thank You that You care for me.
In Jesus' name. Amen.

Open the Door

W)e get ourselves into all kinds of bad situations in our lives and then expect God to come charging in like the cavalry and rescue us. Well, friend, you need to come to terms with the fact that God respects us too much to do that.

Look what He says in Revelation 3:20: *"Behold, I stand at the door and knock. If anyone hears My voice and opens the door, I will come in to him."*

God has given us freewill, and He will never enter in where He is not invited. Do you want God to help you clean up your mess? Then invite Him in. Better yet, invite Him in *before* you make the mess in the first place.

Father, thank You for giving me choice. I choose You and invite You to be part of every situation I face. In Jesus' name. Amen.

The Sure Thing

*I*f you're like me, friend, you've discovered that there are no "sure things" in life. Anything or anyone we count on—for help, for protection, for provision—has the potential to let us down.

Psalm 33:16-18 points out the futility of relying on others and leads us to the only trustworthy source of help: *"No king is saved by the size of his army; no warrior escapes by his great strength. A horse is a vain hope for deliverance; despite all its great strength it cannot save. But the eyes of the Lord are on those who fear Him."*

Who do you rely on in anxious times? Look to the Lord—He'll be there for you *every* time. As He says in Deuteronomy 31:8, *"And the LORD, He is the One who goes before you. He will be with you, He will not leave you nor forsake you; do not fear nor be dismayed."*

Father, thank You that You will
never let me down or forsake me.
I count on You completely.
In Jesus' name. Amen.

EVERYDAY
in Provision

What Do You Need?

Are you in need of finances, of healing, of help in a relationship, but feel it would be too much to ask of God? Think of it this way, friend: If God loves you so very much that He gave His only Son for you, is there *anything* that He would hold back?

Romans 8:32 sets the record straight. *"He who did not spare His own Son, but gave Him up for us all—how will He not also, along with Him, graciously give us all things?"*

Go to your Father and tell Him what you need. You can never ask God for too much—He loves you. He encourages you to ask.

---

*Lord, thank You that You gave me
your very best, and because of that,
You will give me all the rest as well.
In Jesus' name. Amen.*

The Bank of Heaven

omeone once said that time flies. Well friend, in truth, money is a much better aviator. How you look at your money has a lot to do with how useful it is to you.

Proverbs 23:4-5 says something amazing: *"Do not wear yourself out to get rich; have the wisdom to show restraint. Cast but a glance at riches, and they are gone, for they shall surely sprout wings and fly off into the sky like an eagle."*

Money is not an evil thing in itself—but if you have problems with money, maybe it's because you've let it become your priority. Set your focus on the Lord instead—let Him be your banker.

Lord, I place my finances in Your
capable hands—thank You for
always giving me more than enough.
In Jesus' name. Amen.

Give It Away

H ave you ever watched a chipmunk hoarding nuts for the winter? He stores away every morsel of food he can find, hiding it from all the other chipmunks. We tend to do the same thing, my friend—God bestows us with His wonderful gifts, and we hide them away.

2 Corinthians 1:3-4 tells us that God's economy is very different from ours. *"Blessed be...the Father of mercies and God of all comfort, who comforts us in all our tribulation, that we may be able to comfort those who are in any trouble..."*

God gives us gifts in order for us to pass them on, to give them away. The more we give to others, the more God gives back to us. What you make happen for others, God will make happen for you.

---

*Father, thank you that as I give
away what You give to me, I will
never run out. Help me to be a river
of Your gifts, and not a dam.
In Jesus' name. Amen.*

Take the Test Drive

he most exciting part of buying a new car is taking a test drive. It's a chance to experience all the benefits for yourself. Well, did you know that God invites *us* to take a test drive?

His offer is in Malachi 3:10: ***"Bring the whole tithe into the storehouse…Test me in this,' says the Lord Almighty, 'And see if I will not throw open the floodgates of heaven and pour out so much blessing that you will not have room enough for it.'"***

That's quite an offer! "Try Me out," God says. "You bring the tithe, and I'll bless you with more than you can handle."

---

*I will take Your test drive, Father,
and take You at Your Word. Thank
You that I can never out give You.
In Jesus' name. Amen.*

Hindsight

 t's true, you know—hindsight is 20/20. When you look back, how many times have you made plans, only to have them all fall apart—yet the end result was better than you ever could have hoped?

Proverbs 16:9 puts it this way: ***"In his heart a man plans his course, but the Lord determines his steps."***

So, should we even bother to make plans? Yes, absolutely. Just make sure you include God in your planning—and allow Him to make changes. After all, He knows you so much better than you know yourself.

---

*Thank You, Father, that You don't
need hindsight—You see my past,
present, and future. Help me to
include You in all my plans.
In Jesus' name. Amen.*

Heavenly Economics

'm sure you've noticed by now that God's way of doing things is certainly different from our way. Man says, "If you need something, hold on to what you've got, and go get more." God says, "If you need something, give it away, and *I'll* give you more."

God spells out *His* plan for provision in Luke 6:38: *"Give, and it will be given to you: good measure, pressed down, shaken together, and running over will be put into your bosom. For with the same measure that you use, it will be measured back to you."*

If you need a friend, be a friend. If you need money, give money. If you need help, help someone else. When you do, God pours it all back to you.

I'll tell you what, friend—I much prefer God's economy.

Father, I look to You for my
provision. As I give, I know
You will give back to me.
In Jesus' name. Amen.

Twenty-One

The Past Has Passed

he best thing about the past is that it has *passed*. Everything you've done, everything that has happened is over, finished, behind you. Before you is a clean slate, a fresh start— a new beginning in Christ every moment is "now."

Galatians 5:1 talks about God's great gift of "now." *"Stand fast therefore in the liberty by which Christ has made us free, and do not be entangled again with a yoke of bondage."*

That's sound advice, friend: Don't look back. Stand firm in the "now" of God's liberty, His provision, His protection. In this very moment you have <u>all</u> you need to make it to the next moment.

Father, I choose to look forward,
not backward. Thank You
for taking my past and for
giving me a bright future.
In Jesus' name. Amen.

EVERY DAY
in Relationship

Flip Side

F lip a coin—you'll either get heads or tails, but you can't have one without the other. The same is true of the wonderful freedom we have in Christ—there's another side to that coin. The flipside of liberty is responsibility.

Galatians 5:13 puts it this way—*"For you, brethren, have been called to liberty; only do not use liberty as an opportunity for the flesh, but through love serve one another."*

Yes, Jesus has made you truly free, my friend—but the real measure of a man or woman is what you do with that freedom.

---

*Thank you, Lord, for shedding
your blood to make me free—
and help me not to use that freedom
to indulge my own needs,
but as the power to help others.
In Jesus' name. Amen.*

Twenty-Three

Flaming Hoops

ver go to the circus? I was always amazed watching the animals jump through flaming hoops. They would do it just to make their trainers happy. Sometimes we do the same thing: We go to great lengths just to try and please someone else.

Proverbs 29:25 reminds us: ***"The fear of man brings a snare, but whoever trusts in the Lord shall be safe."***

Friend, it's a trap to be worried about what other people think and to let them make you jump through flaming hoops to please them. People can never make us happy or fulfilled—we need to be God-pleasers, not man-pleasers.

Heavenly Father, teach me
that true joy comes from You
and not from trying to please
other people. Set me free from
the flaming hoops in my life.
In Jesus' name. Amen.

Twenty-Four

Spring Cleaning

W e all have that one closet at home that's a catchall for any stray item in the house—it's full of every conceivable piece of junk we've collected over the years. And we certainly don't want any of our friends to see the horrible mess in there.

Matthew 12:34 tells us that our heart is like that closet. *"For out of the abundance of the heart the mouth speaks."*

Friend, you need to keep the closet of your heart clean, because there's no way to hide what's in there—every time you speak or act, you throw open the door for all to see.

Father, help me to keep my heart
clean and pure, so that when others
look at me, they see You.
In Jesus' name. Amen.

Twenty-Five

All to Know You

ho is God to you? Is He some cosmic genie who grants wishes? A lucky charm you keep in your pocket, just in case? A holy slot machine who pays out promises, protection, and provision when you pull the right lever?

John 3:16, the most familiar verse in the Bible, puts it all into perspective: *"For God so loved the world that He gave His only begotten Son, that whoever believes in Him should not perish but have everlasting life."*

You see, friend, all of the gifts and grace God gives to you is for one purpose only—to build a personal relationship with you.

Lord, help me not to look at Your
gifts, but to You, the Gift Giver.
I want to know You, Father.
In Jesus' name. Amen.

Twenty-Six

He Knows Your Name

t's an exciting experience when someone famous knows your name...when you get a personal autograph from a star...a big politician calls you by name...the head of the company recognizes you personally. It makes you feel important and special.

Isaiah 43:1 speaks of the best recognition of all. *"Fear not, for I have redeemed you; I have called you by your name; you are Mine."*

Meditate on that, friend—the God of the universe knows YOUR name and has called you into a personal relationship with Him. That makes you *very* special.

*Father, thank You for calling me
by name. I respond to Your call
by giving You my life.
In Jesus' name. Amen.*

Twenty-Seven

Stubborn as a Mule

ave you ever gone horseback riding? A well-trained animal will respond simply to your voice and a gentle touch. But so many horses are stubborn and require harsher treatment to do what their master wants.

Psalm 32:9 asks which kind of horse you are: *"Do not be like the horse or the mule, which have no understanding and must be controlled by bit and bridle or they will not come to you."*

God's purpose will always prevail. We can choose the easy way and respond to His voice and gentle touch, <u>or</u> we can choose the hard way.

---

*Father, help me to give up
my stubborn ways and obey
Your gentle, loving voice.
In Jesus' name. Amen.*

Twenty-Eight

Listen Twice,
Speak Once

 omeone once said that God gave us two ears and only one mouth so we would listen twice as much as we speak. There's a good reason for that—the more we listen, the more we learn.

And in the meantime, Proverbs 17:28 tells of yet another benefit to listening more than we speak: ***"Even a fool is thought wise if he keeps silent, and discerning if he holds his tongue."***

Friend, we can learn a lot more about most everything if we will listen twice as much as we speak.

Lord, help me to be a good listener,
especially when You are talking to
me. Make me a truly wise person.
In Jesus' name. Amen.

Twenty-Nine

Talk Is Not Cheap

id your parents ever threaten to "wash your mouth out with soap" for something you said? Well, we all need to heed that warning—especially as adults—to clean up our acts and wash out our mouths with the Word of God.

Ephesians 4:29 is just the cleanser we need. *"Do not let any unwholesome talk come out of your mouths, but only what is helpful for building others up according to their needs, that it may benefit those who listen."*

The Bible says we will have to account for every word we speak, so we should make our words count and only say things that will encourage and uplift.

Father, help me to think before I speak, and always keep my mouth clean with Your Word. In Jesus' name. Amen.

It's Your Call

Ever explain something to someone on a cell phone, only to find out that you were accidentally cut off, and they didn't hear a word you said? It happens all the time. But do you sometimes feel that way about God—like you've lost your connection with Him—and that no matter how hard you pray, it seems like He's just not listening?

We've all felt that way, but friend, Psalm 3:4 tells us that our connection is rock-solid. *"I cried to the Lord with my voice...and He heard me."*

Go ahead...pour out your heart to the Lord. He's listening—and more than that—He'll answer you.

---

*Father, I thank You that You
are always there, always listening,
always waiting for me.
In Jesus' name. Amen.*

Thirty-One

Words of Fire

ave you ever seen the devastation of a forest fire? Thousands and thousands of acres can be destroyed—and all from a single, tiny match. The Bible tells us that our tongues are like that match—our words can create tremendous devastation in the hearts and lives of others.

Proverbs 21:23 reminds us that *"Whoever guards his mouth and tongue, keeps his soul from troubles."*

We need to watch what we say, friend—it'll save us from a lot of trouble and make our lives so much easier.

———————— ♪ ————————

Lord, taming my tongue may be
the most difficult thing I ever do—
but with You, all things are possible.
Give me the wisdom to only say
things that will build up others.
In Jesus' name. Amen.

GOD'S ANSWERS
for Your Times of Trouble

When I am afraid, who will protect me?

I will love you, O Lord, my strength. The Lord is my rock and my fortress and my deliverer; My God, my strength, in whom I will trust; my shield and the horn of my salvation, my stronghold. I will call upon the Lord, who is worthy to be praised; so shall I be saved from my enemies.

꙳ PSALM 18:1-3

The angel of the Lord encamps all around those who fear Him, and delivers them.

꙳ PSALM 34:7

When you pass through the waters, I will be with you; and through the rivers, they shall not overflow you. When you walk through the fire, you shall not be burned, nor shall the flame scorch you. For I am the Lord your God, the Holy One of Israel, your Savior.

꙳ ISAIAH 43:2-3

The Lord your God is in your midst, the Mighty One, will save; He will rejoice over you with gladness, He will quiet you with His love, He will rejoice over you with singing.

꙳ ZEPHANIAH 3:17

You are my hiding place; You shall preserve me from trouble; You shall surround me with songs of deliverance.

꙳ PSALM 32:7

When I am anxious, who cares for me?

For You, Lord, are good and ready to forgive, and abundant in lovingkindness to all who call upon You.

ᚱ PSALM 86:5

'For the mountains may be removed and the hills may shake, but My lovingkindness will not be removed from you, and My covenant of peace will not be shaken,' says the Lord who has compassion on you.

ᚱ ISAIAH 54:10

For I am persuaded that neither death nor life, nor angels nor principalities, nor things present nor things to come, nor height nor depth, nor any other created thing, shall be able to separate us from the love of God which is in Christ Jesus our Lord.

ᚱ ROMANS 8:38-39

The Lord appeared to him from afar, saying, 'I have loved you with an everlasting love; therefore I have drawn you with lovingkindness.'

ᚱ JEREMIAH 31:3

But God, who is rich in mercy, because of His great love with which He loved us, even when we were dead in trespasses, made us alive together with Christ (by grace you have been saved).

ᚱ EPHESIANS 2: 4-5

Who can I trust?

Behold, God is my salvation, I will trust and not be afraid; for YAH, the Lord, is my strength and my song; He also has become my salvation.

ॐ ISAIAH 12:2

Be anxious for nothing, but in everything, by prayer and supplication, with thanksgiving, let your request be made known to God; and the peace of God, which surpasses all understanding, will guard your hearts and minds through Christ Jesus.

ॐ PHILIPPIANS 4:6-7

Trust in the Lord with all your heart, and lean not on your own understanding; in all your ways acknowledge Him, and He shall direct your paths.

ॐ PROVERBS 3:5-6

Blessed is the man who trusts in the Lord, and whose hope is in the Lord.

ॐ JEREMIAH 17:7

Trust in the Lord and do good; dwell in the land, and feed on His faithfulness. Delight yourself also in the Lord, and He shall give you the desires of your heart. Commit your way to the Lord, trust also in Him, and He shall bring it to pass.

ॐ PSALM 37: 3-5

Where is my peace?

ave I not commanded you? Be strong and of good courage; do not be afraid, nor be dismayed, for the Lord your God is with you wherever you go.

JOSHUA 1:9

ou will keep him in perfect peace, whose mind is stayed on you, because he trusts in You. Trust in the Lord forever, for in YAH the Lord, is everlasting strength.

ISAIAH 26:3-4

eace I leave with you. My peace I give to you; not as the world gives do I give to you. Let not your heart be troubled, neither let it be afraid.

JOHN 14:27

or God has not given us a spirit of fear, but of power and of love and of a sound mind.

2 TIMOTHY 1:7

n the day when I cried out, You answered me, and made me bold with strength in my soul.

PSALM 138:3

When I don't know what to do, where do I turn?

I will instruct you and teach you in the way you should go; I will guide you with My eye.

✤ PSALM 32:8

*Y*et they will by no means follow a stranger, but will flee from him, for they do not know the voice of a stranger…My sheep hear My voice, and I know them, and they follow me.

✤ JOHN 10:5, 27

*I*f any of you lacks wisdom, let him ask of God, who gives to all liberally and without reproach, and it will be given to him.

✤ JAMES 1:5

*S*how me Your ways, O Lord; teach me Your paths. Lead me in Your truth and teach me, for You are the God of my salvation; on You I wait all the day.

✤ PSALM 25:4-5

*A*ll Scripture is given by inspiration of God, and is profitable for doctrine, for reproof, for correction, for instruction in righteousness, that the man of God may be complete, thoroughly equipped for every good work.

✤ 2 TIMOTHY 3:16-17

God Answers Prayer!

"If two of you agree on earth concerning anything that they ask, it will be done for them by My Father in Heaven."
— MATTHEW 18:19

"Thanks so much for your prayers for my husband Michael, who had been diagnosed with cancer. Michael went back for a check-up, and the doctor said his cancer is GONE! Praise the Lord!" — HELEN

"Your prayers and those of our friends have brought Divine healing to my mom's thyroid disease! She's returned to her former health!" — JAMES

"My wife's back was healed when your prayer minister agreed with me in prayer!" — ALLEN

"Thank you for your prayers! I've received a total healing regarding high blood pressure and a possible stroke." — IBIRONKE

Our prayer ministers welcome the opportunity to agree together with you in prayer and believe God to step into the circumstances of your life with His supernatural power!

In the U.S., call 803-578-1800 7 days a week, 24 hours a day.
In the U.K., call 0845 683 0584 Monday – Friday, 09:30 – 21:30.
Or email your prayer request to Prayer@inspiration.org.

"Thank you for having one of your Prayer Ministers call and pray with me today. The call came at just the right time, and it made me feel like someone really cares.
— GLORIA

Inspiration
PROMISE BOOK

This beautiful, plush-covered, 242-page book is a...

- Guide to help you pray for your loved ones
- Daily Devotional tool to bring you closer to the Lord
- Powerful manual for spiritual warfare

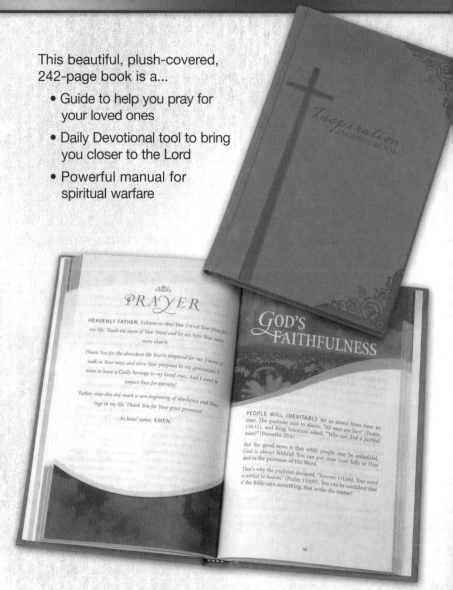

BE BLESSED!

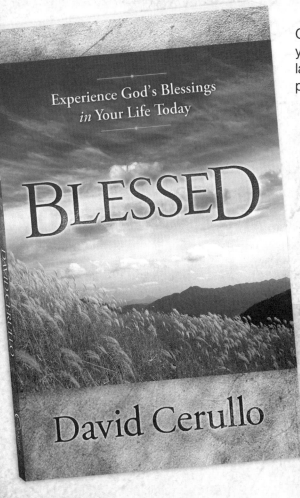

Experience God's Blessings *in* Your Life Today

BLESSED

David Cerullo

God wants to bless you abundantly! My latest book, ***Blessed***, provides you with...

- 12 life-changing "Blessing Keys"
- A simple equation to release God's abundance
- Fresh insights on God's powerful principles of Seedtime and Harvest

"I will bless you...and you shall be a blessing."
–Genesis 12:2

Souls and receive one or more of these life-changing
us to impact people for Christ worldwide!

Do You Need a MIRACLE From God?

God is a God of MIRACLES!

Do you need God's supernatural intervention today in your...

- **BODY, SOUL, OR SPIRIT?**
- **FINANCES, HOME, OR JOB?**
- **RELATIONSHIPS WITH LOVED ONES?**

This life-changing ministry resource will help you experience the miracle you need from Him!

"How to Receive Your Miracle tells me how to look forward to God's promises for complete healing in my life. This book has been an eye opener for me to the keys of living!" — KAREN

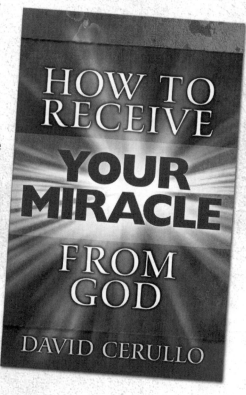

HOW TO RECEIVE YOUR MIRACLE FROM GOD

DAVID CERULLO

Visit www.inspiration.org, or call 866-324-5001 *ministry tools as a "Thank You" gift for partneri*

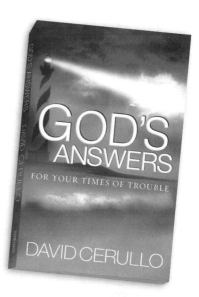